GODS & GODDESSES
OF THE ANCIENT WORLD

Ra

BY VIRGINIA LOH-HAGAN

Gods and goddesses were the main characters of myths. Myths are traditional stories from ancient cultures. Storytellers answered questions about the world by creating exciting explanations. People thought myths were true. Myths explained the unexplainable. They helped people make sense of human behavior and nature. Today, we use science to explain the world. But people still love myths. Myths may not be literally true. But they have meaning. They tell us something about our history and culture.

Published in the United States of America by Cherry Lake Publishing
Ann Arbor, Michigan
www.cherrylakepublishing.com

Reading Adviser: Marla Conn, MS, Ed., Literacy specialist, Read-Ability, Inc.
Book Design: Jen Wahi

Photo Credits: ©Howard David Johnson, 2019, cover, 1, 12; ©OlgaKot17/Shutterstock, 5; ©Elena Puchkina/Shutterstock, 6; ©Merydolla/Shutterstock, 9; ©Africa Studio/Shutterstock, 11; ©Elenarts/Shutterstock, 15; ©forgetselfies/Shutterstock, 17; ©Oksana Galiulina/Shutterstock, 19; ©agsaz/Shutterstock, 21; ©Jagoush/Shutterstock, 22; ©Stig Alenas/Shutterstock, 25; ©DrObjektiff/Shutterstock, 27; ©Vladimir Zadvinskii/Shutterstock, 29

Library of Congress Cataloging-in-Publication Data

Names: Loh-Hagan, Virginia, author. | Loh-Hagan, Virginia. Gods & goddesses of the ancient world.
Title: Ra / written by Virginia Loh-Hagan.
Description: Ann Arbor, Michigan : Cherry Lake Publishing, 2019. | Series: Gods and goddesses of the ancient world
Identifiers: LCCN 2019004212 | ISBN 9781534147720 (hardcover) | ISBN 9781534149151 (pdf) | ISBN 9781534150584 (pbk.) | ISBN 9781534152014 (hosted ebook)
Subjects: LCSH: Ra (Egyptian deity)—Juvenile literature. | Gods, Egyptian—Juvenile literature. | Mythology, Egyptian—Juvenile literature.
Classification: LCC BL2450.R2 L64 2019 | DDC 299/.312113—dc23
LC record available at https://lccn.loc.gov/2019004212

Printed in the United States of America
Corporate Graphics

ABOUT THE AUTHOR:

Dr. Virginia Loh-Hagan is an author, university professor, former classroom teacher, and curriculum designer. She lives in a very sunny city! She lives in San Diego with her very tall husband and very naughty dogs. To learn more about her, visit www.virginialoh.com.

TABLE OF CONTENTS

CHAPTER 1

GOD OF GODS

Who is Ra? What does he look like?

Ra was an **ancient** Egyptian god. Ancient means old. Egypt is a country in the Middle East. It's in North Africa.

Ancient Egyptians honored Ra. Ra was the Sun God. He gave light. He gave warmth.

He was a member of the Great Ennead. The Ennead were the 9 most important gods and goddesses. This group was the original gods and goddesses of ancient Egypt. Ra ruled over all the gods. He also ruled the sky. He ruled the earth. He ruled the **underworld**. The underworld is the place where dead people's souls go.

Ancient Egyptians believed that a piece of Ra was in all the gods and goddesses.

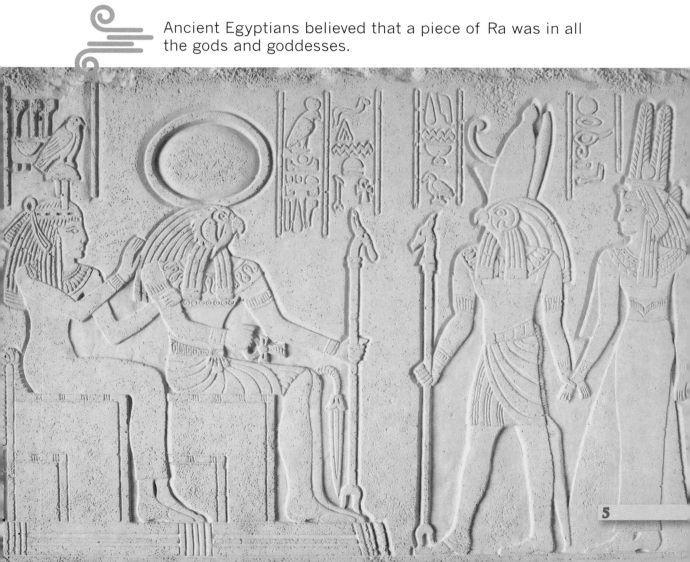

Ra watched everyone from the sky. On earth, Horus ruled on his behalf.

Ra took many forms. He was a hawk god. He had the head of a hawk. He had the body of a human. Sometimes, he appeared as a man. Sometimes, he turned into a hawk. He also used the head of a beetle or a **ram**. Rams are male sheep. Ra took on other animal forms. Examples are snakes, bulls, cats, or lions.

Ra wore a fancy **headdress**. Headdresses are head coverings. Ra wore a **solar disc**. Solar means sun. Disc is a flat circle. A snake was wrapped around the disc.

In some stories, Ra was an aging ruler. He had golden skin. He had silver bones. He had hair of blue gems.

Family Tree

Parent: Nun (water of disorder)

Children: Shu (god of light and dry air) and Tefnut (goddess of wet air and rain)

Grandchildren: Geb (god of the earth) and Nut (goddess of the sky)

Great-grandchildren: Osiris (god of the afterlife, underworld, and rebirth), Set (god of disorder and deserts), Nephthys (goddess of darkness and water), and Isis (goddess of marriage, fertility, motherhood, magic, and medicine)

CHAPTER 2

CREATOR GOD

How is Ra born? How does Ra create the world?

Ra was a **creator god**. This means he made the world. As the sun, Ra had great power. Ancient Egyptians needed the sun to live. This made Ra very important. Ra was the center of everything. This is just like the sun.

Before Ra, the world was crazy. Nun was the first waters. He was the water of **chaos**. Chaos means disorder. Nun was like Ra's father. Ra created himself from Nun's waters.

He emerged as a mound of dirt. This mound was shaped like an egg. Sunlight hit the mound. It gave the dirt power. Ra came up from the waters. He rose. The dirt became Ra.

Pyramids were believed to look like Ra's mound of dirt.

All in the Family

Tefnut was the goddess of wet air and rain. Her name means "she of water." Tefnut married her twin brother, Shu. Her father was Ra. Tefnut was a member of the Ennead. She's an important goddess. She has a human body. She has the head of a lioness. Sometimes, she takes the form of a snake with a lion's head. Ancient Egyptians prayed to her. They prayed for the health of their leaders. Tefnut could be bitter. One time, she got mad at Ra. She wanted to punish him. She left Egypt. She took all the water with her. This dried up the land. People suffered. They couldn't grow crops. They were hungry. They starved. Meanwhile, Tefnut took lion form. She traveled around. Ra sent for her. Tefnut returned. She brought back the water. She made the Nile River flood. This made people happy.

Ancient Egyptian gods married their own family members. They did this to keep royal blood in the family.

Ra spit. His spit became Tefnut. Tefnut was the goddess of wet air and rain. She brought water to the world. Ra sneezed. His sneeze became Shu. Shu was the god of light and dry air. He brought winds.

Tefnut and Shu were twins. They married each other. They had children. Ra's children and grandchildren helped create the rest of the world.

Ra made the seasons. He made months. He created all forms of life. He called them to life. He said their secret names. Only he knew their names. Ra made plants. He made animals. Everything was perfect. It was so beautiful.

Ra was happy. He cried tears of joy. His tears hit the earth. His tears became humans. Ra shined his light. This gave humans life. Ancient Egyptians called themselves the "**cattle** of Ra." Cattle are tamed cows.

Ra cut himself. He bled. His blood turned into powers. Examples are Hu and Sia. Hu was command. Sia was intelligence. Hu and Sia helped humans rule themselves. Ra also gave humans leadership. His great-great-grandchild was Horus. Horus was the god of kings. He lived through the **pharaohs**. Pharaohs are ancient Egyptian rulers.

 Some stories say Ra's sweat became humans as well.

CHAPTER 3

SUN GOD

How does Ra move the sun? Who is his enemy?

Ra lived in the sky. He had a special boat. His boat was called "the boat of millions of years." Ra sailed across the sky. He did this every day.

Ra controlled the sun's movement. In the morning, he sailed from the east. As he sailed, the sun rose. Ra carried the prayers and blessings of the living. He sailed his boat toward the west. It took him all day to do this. As he sailed, the sun went down.

At the end of the day, Ra died. He was swallowed by Nut. Nut was his granddaughter. She was the goddess of the sky.

Ra sailed into the underworld. He left the moon in the sky. This is so humans had some light. Ra fought against

Ra had a night boat and a day boat.

monsters. He visited dead souls. He gave them messages from the living. He sailed back to Nut. Every dawn, Nut gave birth to Ra.

Ra's main enemy was Apep. Apep was an evil snake. He was the lord of chaos. He was born from Ra's belly button. He tried to stop Ra's boat. He did this every day. Ra fought him every day. He did this as he sailed. Sometimes, Ra turned into a cat. He attacked Apep. Sunny days meant Ra won. Stormy days meant Apep won.

Ancient Egyptians loved cats.

CHAPTER 4

SUN POWER

What is the Eye of Ra? What is the Tree of Life? What is Bennu?

Ra's sun disc was known as the Eye of Ra. This was his source of sun power. It contained sunlight, warmth, and energy. All of these things are needed for life. They're needed to grow food. But the sun disc could also be dangerous. The sun burns. It destroys. It dries up the land. Its heat could be very strong in Egypt. Some ancient Egyptians thought sun rays were Ra's arrows.

The Eye of Ra also referred to goddesses. These goddesses served as Ra's eyes. They watched over things for him. They did things in his name.

Ancient Egyptians used the sun disc for protection.

Real World Connection

Bertrand Piccard was born in Switzerland. He came from a family of explorers. His grandfather rode hot air balloons. His father was an undersea explorer. Piccard is also an explorer. He created the Solar Impulse. Solar Impulse is a special aircraft. It's powered by the sun. It doesn't use any gas. It was used to travel around the world. This was the first successful solar-powered flight around the world. This happened in 2016. It took about 14 months. It took 550 hours in the air. It traveled 25,000 miles (40,234 kilometers) around the world. It crossed 4 continents. It crossed 2 oceans. It crossed 3 seas. Piccard said, "Everyone said it was impossible. [They] said I was just dreaming." The aircraft was designed very carefully. It needed to be big enough to hold solar panels. But it needed to be light enough to fly. Its wings couldn't tip very far. Winds could take the aircraft off course.

The Tree of Life was in Ra's temple. Temples are buildings of worship.

Ra is also connected to the Tree of Life. This tree grew from Nun's waters. It grew on Ra's mound of dirt. Its branches reached out to the sky. The branches held up the stars. The tree's roots reached down to the underworld. The trunk was the world's **pillar**. Pillar means large post. The trunk held the world together.

The tree was **sacred**. Sacred means godly. Only gods and pharaohs could use the tree. Humans could not. The tree

Sometimes, Ra took the form of a phoenix.

made special fruit. Gods and pharaohs who ate the fruit would have eternal life. They would never die. They would never get old. Eternal means forever.

Bennu lived in the Tree of Life. He was a **phoenix**. A phoenix is a **mythical** bird. Mythical means not real. A phoenix lived for hundreds of years. It set itself on fire. It burned into ashes. It rose from its own ashes. It kept on living in this way. A phoenix represents rebirth. It represents creation. This is like Ra.

Bennu was believed to be Ra's soul. He flew over Nun's waters. He landed on the Tree of Life. He said the word "creation." He inspired Ra to be a creator god. He inspired him to use his body parts to create the world.

Cross-Cultural Connection

Amaterasu was a sun goddess. She ruled the heavens. She was worshipped by the Japanese. Her name means "shining in heaven." Japanese emperors got their power from her. Emperors are rulers. They're like pharaohs. Amaterasu was born when her father washed out his left eye. She was the sister of Susanoo and Tsukuyomi. Susanoo was the god of storms and seas. Tsukuyomi was the god of the moon. The three of them made the world. Amaterasu and Tsukuyomi fought. This made night and day. Amaterasu broke Susanoo's sword into 3 pieces. This made 3 female goddesses. Susanoo ate Amaterasu's necklace. He spit it out. He made 5 male gods. These 8 gods and goddesses became the first Japanese nobles. Nobles are leaders.

CHAPTER 5

SUN SECRETS

What is a story about Ra's eye? How does Ra create death? How does Isis trick Ra?

There's a story about Ra's eye. One day, Shu and Tefnut left Ra. This made Ra mad. Ra wanted to find them. He took out his eye. He sent his eye to find his children. His eye did just that. Then, it brought Shu and Tefnut back to Ra.

But without his eye, Ra wasn't as strong. During this time, he was weak. He was not as powerful. His enemies could attack him. Some people believe this is the reason for solar eclipses. Solar eclipses are when the moon blocks out the sun's light.

There's a story about Ra creating death. At first, Ra loved humans. Then, he hated them. He saw all the mean things humans did. He got mad. He sent for Sekhmet to punish humans. Sekhmet was made from the fire in Ra's eye.

When Ra lost his eye, other gods helped him find it.

Ra changed Sekhmet into a lioness. He sent her to earth. He told her to kill humans. Sekhmet went crazy. She killed a lot of people. Ra changed his mind. He wanted to save some humans. He tricked Sekhmet. He gave her a red drink. Sekhmet thought it was blood. The drink made her sleepy. Sekhmet stopped killing. Death was now introduced into the world.

There's a story about Isis tricking Ra. Isis was the goddess of magic. She wanted Ra's power. She needed Ra's secret name to get his power. Ra became an old man. He drooled. Spit came out of his mouth. His spit fell to earth. Isis took his spit. She mixed it with dirt. She rolled it. She shaped it. She made a snake. She put the snake in Ra's path. The snake bit Ra. Ra felt death. He asked Isis for help. Isis made a deal.

 Ra's Golden Age ended when death was introduced.

Explained By Science

The sun is a big star. There are over 100 billion stars in the universe. The sun is at the center of our solar system. Earth and other planets circle the sun. The sun holds the solar system together. It gives light. It gives heat. It gives energy. It makes space weather. It's filled with hot gases. It's extremely hot. Light carries energy to the top layer. Boiling motions of gases move the heat to the surface. This takes over a million years to happen. The sun also makes wind. The wind blows very quickly. The sun is over 4.6 billion years old. Many scientists think the sun and the rest of the solar system formed from a nebula. A nebula is a big cloud of gas and dust. There was a big bang. This made the nebula spin and become flat. Material pulled toward the center. This formed the sun.

The Eye of Ra represents many things. One thing it represents is the sun's great heat.

Ra told her his secret name. Isis healed him. But she took his powers.

Don't anger the gods. Ra had great powers. And he knew how to use them.

DID YOU KNOW?

- Pharaohs are ancient Egyptian rulers. They got their powers from gods and goddesses. King Tut was a famous ancient Egyptian pharaoh. He was named after Ra. Ra was also known as Atum-Ra or Amun-Ra. King Tut's full name was Tutankhamun. This means "living form of Amun."

- Ancient Egyptians worshipped Ra. They built solar temples for him. Solar means sun. These temples didn't have statues of Ra. Instead, they were open. They let sunlight in. Ra was the sunlight. The earliest temple was built in Cairo. It's called Benu-Phoenix. It's supposed to be the exact spot where Ra was created. Cairo is the capital of Egypt. It used to be called Heliopolis. This means the "city of the sun."

- Ancient Egyptians were famous for building pyramids. Pyramids are buildings. They look like triangles. These pyramids represent sun rays. They were built for pharaohs. They were tombs. This connected Ra to pharaohs.

- Ancient Romans conquered Egypt. They did this around 30 BCE. This is when people stopped believing in Ra. Instead, they started to believe in Judaism and Christianity. Judaism and Christianity are religions. These religions believe in one God. Ancient Egyptians believed in many gods and goddesses.

- Some people still believe in ancient Egyptian gods and goddesses. They worship Ra as the supreme god of the sun. Their religion is called Kemetism. What's old is new again!

- In some stories, Ra changed forms as the sun. When he was rising, he was a beetle. When he was setting, he was a ram. At noon, he was Ra. This is when the sun is the most powerful.

CONSIDER THIS!

TAKE A POSITION! Read the 45th Parallel Press series on Egyptian gods and goddesses. Some people think Ra is the most important god. What do you think? Which god is most important and why? Argue your point with reasons and evidence.

SAY WHAT? Read the 45th Parallel Press book about Horus. In some stories, Horus and Ra are the same god. Explain how they're alike. Explain how they're different.

THINK ABOUT IT! Ra had several animal forms. Why do you think gods are connected to animals? If you could take on an animal form, what would it be? Why did you choose that animal?

LEARN MORE

Braun, Eric. *Egyptian Myths*. North Mankato, MN: Capstone Press, 2019.

Napoli, Donna Jo, and Christina Balit (illust.). *Treasury of Egyptian Mythology: Classic Stories of Gods, Goddesses, Monsters, and Mortals*. Washington, DC: National Geographic Kids, 2013.

Reinhart, Matthew, and Robert Sabuda. *Gods and Heroes*. Somerville, MA: Candlewick Press, 2010.

GLOSSARY

ancient (AYN-shuhnt) old, from a long time ago

cattle (KAT-uhl) tamed cows

chaos (KAY-ahs) disorder

creator god (kree-AY-tur GAHD) god who created the world and humans

disc (DISK) flat circle

headdress (HED-dres) a fancy head covering

mythical (MITH-ih-kuhl) magical, not real, fictional, only existing in stories

pharaohs (FAIR-ohz) ancient Egyptian rulers

phoenix (FEE-nix) a mythical bird that lived for hundreds of years by setting itself on fire and rising from its own ashes

pillar (PIL-ur) a large post used to support a structure

ram (RAM) male sheep

sacred (SAY-krid) godly

solar (SOH-lur) sun

underworld (UHN-dur-wurld) the land of the dead

INDEX